PIONEERS OF SCIENCE

GUGLIELMO MARCONI

Nina Morgan

921
MAR

The Bookwright Press
New York • 1991

Pioneers of Science

Alexander Graham Bell
Marie Curie
Michael Faraday
Guglielmo Marconi
Isaac Newton
Leonardo da Vinci

First published in the
United States in 1991 by
The Bookwright Press
387 Park Avenue South
New York, NY 10016

First published in 1990 by
Wayland (Publishers) Limited
61 Western Road, Hove
East Sussex BN3 1JD, England

Library of Congress Cataloging–in–Publication Data
    Guglielmo Marconi / by Nina Morgan.
        p. cm. — (Pioneers of science)
    Includes bibliographical references and index.
    Summary: Discusses the visionary inventor's life, his application of
theories in physics to discover radio, and his contributions to the science
of communication.
    ISBN 0–531–18417–X
    1. Marconi, Guglielmo, marchese, 1874–1937—Juvenile literature.
2. Inventors—Italy—Biography—Juvenile literature. 3. Marconi,
Guglielmo, marchese, 1874–1937. [1. Inventors.] I. Title. II. Series.
TK5739.M3M67 1991
621.384'092—dc20
[B]
[92]   90–1268
                                                           CIP
                                                            AC

Typeset by Rachel Gibbs, Wayland
Printed in Italy by Rotolito Lombarda S.p.A.

Contents

1 ▽ Introduction

When Guglielmo (pronounced "Gwe-yel-mo") Marconi was born on April 25, 1874, all the servants in his father's large house in Bologna, Italy, crowded into his mother's bedroom to welcome the new baby. As they stood in admiration, the old gardener suddenly exclaimed, "What big ears he has!" Guglielmo's mother replied with a smile, "He will be able to hear the still small voice of the air." Little did she realize how true her words would prove to be, for when Guglielmo was born, the age of modern communications was just beginning. By the time he died, wireless communication around the world was a reality. Its development was largely due to the dreams and the hard work of the little Italian boy with the big ears who grew up to become the inventor of wireless telegraphy, radio and radar.

Communication was very different a hundred and fifty years ago. For most people, long-distance communication meant writing letters. When the Penny Post, the forerunner of our modern postal system,

With the introduction of the Penny Post, letter writing became a popular means of communication. This illustration shows a mail coach traveling through a thunderstorm in southern England.

By 1877 it had become possible to send messages to many places using the telegraph system. This form of communication depends on pulses of electricity traveling along wires. Setting up the wires was a huge task.

began in England in 1840, it became possible for more people to send and receive letters. But even so, for communication over relatively short distances, many people still considered that the quickest and most reliable method was a boy and a pony.

By the mid-1880s things were changing because scientists were beginning to understand more and more about the properties of electricity and how it could be put to use. There were many pioneers in the world of communications, and by 1877 it had become possible to send messages to many places using a telegraph or a telephone.

Both the telephone and the telegraph depend on wires or cables to transmit messages. These cables were often difficult to lay and were easily damaged. Marconi's discovery, that messages could be transmitted without wires, using a type of electromagnetic wave known as a radio wave, led to many new developments in communications.

At first, radio waves were used to provide communication links to places where wires could not reach, such as ships at sea. Then they were applied to telephones; then to the development of radio and television. Now, literally, the sky is the limit. Electromagnetic waves transmitted via satellites permit thousands of messages to be sent at the same time to all parts of the world.

Today radio and television broadcasts provide up-to-date news from all parts of the globe, and talking to someone on the other side of the world is as simple as making a local telephone call. Thanks to the pioneering work of scientists like Guglielmo Marconi, we can all keep in touch.

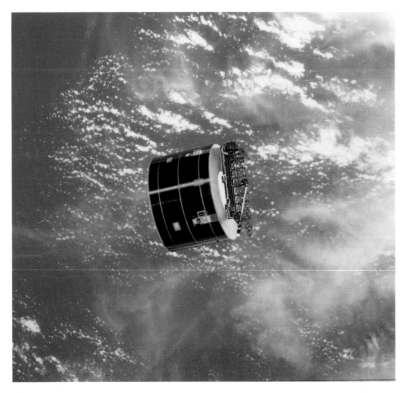

Today electromagnetic waves transmitted via satellites permit messages, as well as radio and television broadcasts, to be sent all over the world.

2 The Boy Who Loved Electricity

Guglielmo Marconi was the third son of Giuseppe Marconi, a successful Italian businessman. Giuseppe was nearly fifty when Guglielmo was born, and he left the raising of his youngest son largely in the hands of his lively young Irish wife, Annie. Guglielmo did not have many companions as a child because his brother, Alphonso, and half-brother, Luigi, were much older and had their own interests. His closest friend was his cousin Daisy, the daughter of his mother's sister, but she came to visit the Marconi family for only a few months each year. The rest of the time Guglielmo was left to his own devices.

The villa Grifone near Bologna, Italy. This lovely house was part of Giuseppe Marconi's country estate. Guglielmo was born here.

The first successful attempt to prove Benjamin Franklin's theory about the relationship between electricity and lightning took place on May 10, 1752, at Marly, near Paris, France.

You might imagine that Guglielmo was lonely because he spent so much of his time by himself. However, he never noticed his isolation because his mind was always teeming with new and exciting ideas. "If only you knew what a lot of ideas I have got in my head!" he once remarked to his cousin Daisy. Guglielmo loved the countryside and the study of nature, and he spent many hours fishing. He also loved to spend time reading in his father's library. At first, books about Greek myths and history were his favorites, but these were soon replaced by books about science.

Guglielmo had two great heroes. The first was Benjamin Franklin, the American statesman and scientist who died in 1790. Franklin once flew a kite with a metal key attached to it in a thunderstorm. When the key was back on the ground, the electric sparks that Franklin drew from it proved that lightning was a form of electricity. His second great hero was Michael Faraday, the English scientist who made many important discoveries about electricity and magnetism. Faraday died seven years before Guglielmo was born.

Electricity soon became Guglielmo's great passion and he often talked to his cousin Daisy about "my electricity." He also loved machinery and delighted in making electrical gadgets. One of his favorites was a zinc structure on the roof of his house, which he wired to a bell indoors. The contraption was designed to catch the static electricity from thunderstorms. Whenever a storm occurred the bell rang indoors – to Guglielmo's great delight.

The English scientist Michael Faraday was one of Guglielmo's childhood heroes. Faraday did much to increase our understanding of electricity and magnetism. He is shown here working in his laboratory.

His mother, Annie, indulged her youngest son and did everything she could to help him in his work, but his father could be very stern. He thought Guglielmo's gadgets were a nuisance and a waste of time. He was very angry when Guglielmo tried to imitate one of Benjamin Franklin's experiments and accidentally demolished a whole row of dinner plates. From then on, he destroyed Guglielmo's experiments whenever he came across them. Guglielmo and his mother teamed up to keep them hidden from him.

Guglielmo did not go to a real school until he was twelve. His first school was in Florence and he disliked it intensely. He felt shy among all the other boys, and they teased him because he could not speak Italian very well.

After this unhappy start at school, Annie took her sons to live in Livorno on the Mediterranean coast of Italy. There, to his father's delight, Guglielmo decided to try to become a naval officer. Unfortunately he failed to qualify for the Naval Academy and once again displeased his father. Giuseppe was convinced that Guglielmo was unsuccessful because he had wasted his time with his scientific "rubbish."

In Morse code, the letters of the alphabet, numbers and punctuation are represented by different patterns of dots and dashes. These can be transmitted over wires by long and short pulses of electricity.

A •—	N —•	1 •——•	. ••——••
B —•••	O ••	2 ••—••	, •—•—
C •• •	P •••••	3 •••—•	? —••—•
D —••	Q ••—•	4 ••••—	: —•— ••
E •	R • ••	5 ———	; ••• ••
F •—•	S •••	6 ••••••	- •••• •—••
G ——•	T —	7 ——••	/ ••— —
H ••••	U ••—	8 —••••	" ••—• —•
I ••	V •••—	9 —••—	
J —•—•	W •——	0 —	
K —•—	X •—••		
L —	Y •• ••		
M ——	Z ••• •		

Samuel Morse's first recording telegraph of 1837 recorded the dots and dashes as a series of peaks and troughs on a line. Other inventors soon developed more sophisticated versions of Morse's original machine.

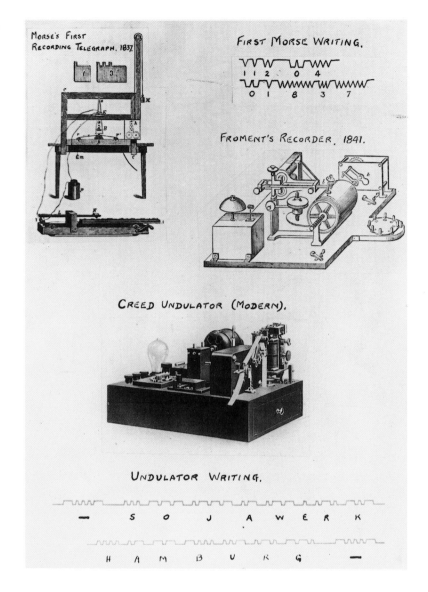

When he was thirteen, Guglielmo attended the Livorno Technical Institute, where he heard formal lectures on physics and chemistry for the first time. From then on he became an eager student and even persuaded his mother to pay for extra lessons so that he could learn the basic laws of electricity. He also made friends with an old, blind telegrapher, who taught him Morse code, a code used for sending messages along telegraph wires. In Morse code, letters are made up of long and short pulses of electricity and are written as a series of dots and dashes. This skill proved very useful to Guglielmo in his later life. Unfortunately, in spite of

Guglielmo with his mother, Annie, and his older brother, Alphonso.

his new dedication to his studies, he could not pass the entrance examination to Bologna University and this angered his father again.

Soon Guglielmo was spending most of his spare time studying and experimenting with electricity. To avoid his father's disapproval, he chose a secret place in the garden to carry out his experiments. His equipment was simple: an old jam jar filled with water and a few strands of wire.

Although he tried to keep his work secret, his experiments were so exciting that he could not resist telling his mother. Although Annie did not really understand what Guglielmo was doing, she was so pleased to see him interested and happy that, without telling her husband, she gave her son an attic room to use as his laboratory. She also persuaded Professor Augustus Righi, a physics lecturer at Bologna University and one of their neighbors, to help him.

Professor Righi allowed Guglielmo to set up experiments in the physics laboratory at the University and to borrow equipment for experiments at home. Guglielmo also visited the University Library, where he read everything he could find about electricity.

Guglielmo was delighted with his attic laboratory, and spent long hours working there. By the time he was eighteen he had accumulated shelves of mysterious apparatus and jars of colored liquids, but he still had not invented anything or made any new scientific discovery. His father eventually discovered the laboratory, and told his son that he was wasting his time. Many others thought so too, but Guglielmo worked on.

Guglielmo Marconi made his first big breakthrough in 1894, when he was nearly twenty. While on vacation in the Alps with his half-brother he read an article about the work of the German physicist Heinrich Hertz. The article described how Hertz had set up an experiment that proved the existence of electromagnetic waves, waves of energy that travel at the velocity of light through a vacuum and can pass through solids, liquids and gases. Guglielmo immediately saw the exciting possibility of using these waves for the sending and receiving of messages without wires. He could hardly wait to return home so that he could shut himself up in his laboratory and work on his idea.

Messages Through the Air

Marconi continued to work long hours in his attic laboratory. In spite of his father's disapproval and refusal to give him money to buy the wire, batteries and sheets of metal he needed for his experiments, he carried on with his work with great determination. One day he even sold his shoes to get money for supplies.

Marconi's teacher, Professor Righi, could not understand how his pupil, who had little formal training in science, could hope to study the uses of electromagnetic waves when none of the great physicists of the day had yet come to understand them. Marconi saw things differently. He did not worry about the fundamental theory of electromagnetic waves; he only cared whether he could find a way to use them to transmit messages over long distances without wires.

Marconi's simple transmitter could send signals over a distance of a few yards. It consisted of two insulated plates separated by a spark gap. The spark gap was formed by two small spheres, linked by a wire but separated by a space. When the power was turned on, an electrical spark jumped across the gap.

Hertz's experiment

Marconi's first aim was to reproduce Hertz's experiment. Hertz had used a simple type of transmitter and receiver system to demonstrate that electromagnetic waves exist. The transmitter was connected to a battery and consisted of a coil of wire attached to two copper plates placed close together but with a small gap between them. The receiver was a copper ring with a gap in it. When Hertz pressed a key he completed the electrical circuit in the transmitter and caused a large spark to jump across the gap. The instant that the spark jumped across the transmitter gap, a tiny spark jumped across the receiver gap, even though it was not connected to the transmitter by wires. This experiment showed that some of the energy supplied to the transmitter must have been radiated as electromagnetic waves and that a small amount of this energy had reached the receiver.

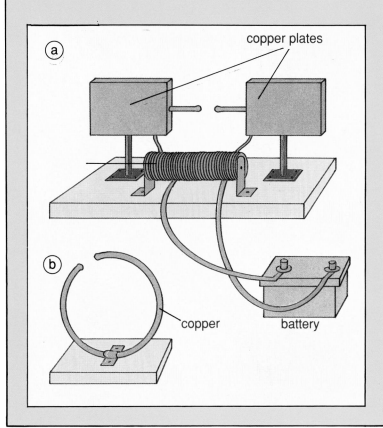

Hertz used a simple type of transmitter (a) and receiver (b) to demonstrate that electromagnetic waves exist. His apparatus is shown here.

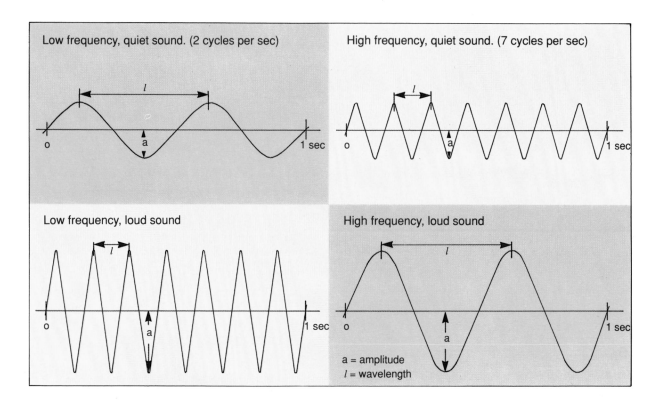

Low frequency, quiet sound. (2 cycles per sec)

High frequency, quiet sound. (7 cycles per sec)

Low frequency, loud sound

High frequency, loud sound

a = amplitude
l = wavelength

Once Marconi had succeeded in reproducing Hertz's experiment and had sent electromagnetic waves over an inch or so, he set about trying to find ways to transmit the waves over longer and longer distances. He became obsessed with his work, and although he had many failures, he was determined never to give up. Eventually he was able to send waves across a room, and to use electromagnetic waves to make an electric bell ring two floors below his laboratory. As exciting as this was, he did not stop there. He continued to make improvements to the receiver and the transmitter so that the waves received at the receiver could be used to run a Morse printing machine. It was now possible to transmit and receive messages in Morse code, without wires.

Next Marconi asked his brother Alphonso to help him try to send signals in the open air. He set up the receiver in the garden a short distance from the house and asked his brother to stand by it and wave a red flag if a signal was received. Marconi rushed to his laboratory and tapped out a series of dots and dashes

A diagram showing the properties of waves: wavelength, frequency and amplitude.

on his transmitter. Almost immediately he saw Alphonso excitedly waving the red flag and he knew his experiment had worked! The two brothers then tried to extend the range farther and farther and eventually transmitted a message from one side of a hill to the other. For this trial, Alphonso had to shoot a gun to tell his brother that the message had been received.

Marconi had been able to achieve these astonishing improvements to his system by making various changes to his receiver and transmitter. He began by using a much more sensitive detector on his receiver. This consisted of a small glass tube filled with metal dust with an electrical contact at each end. When the electromagnetic waves were received they caused the metal dust particles to cling together. This reduced the electrical resistance between the contacts and, as a result, the current flowed more freely. When he connected the detector to a battery and an electric buzzer to a Morse printing machine, he noticed that there was a fall in the electrical resistance. This decrease in resistance led to an increase in the current in the battery circuit and the increased current caused the buzzer to sound or the printer to print.

Marconi's Morse code transmitter and receiver. The message tapped out on the Morse transmitter is transmitted as electro-magnetic waves to the receiver, where they are picked up by means of an antenna.

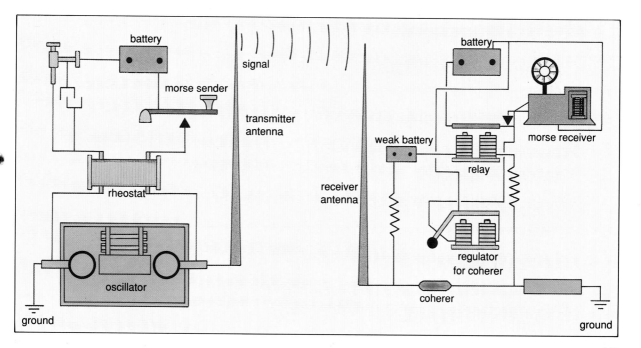

One of Marconi's early receivers. This one was built in 1897, the year after Marconi arrived in England.

Even greater improvements were to come. One day, when Marconi was experimenting with his apparatus in the garden, he decided to add a large metal plate to each side of the spark gap on the transmitter. By chance he happened to hold one of the metal slabs high in the air while the other metal slab rested on the ground. To his surprise and delight he found that the signals became so strong that he could send messages as far as half a mile or more. What he had discovered was the principle of increasing the transmission distance by means of an antenna, or aerial, (the slab held in the air) and a ground (the slab placed on the ground). From then on his progress was rapid and exciting.

Marconi recruited his brother Alphonso and a few of his father's employees to act as assistants. Together they carried out many experiments, each time extending the transmitting distance a little further. Rather than working out theories, Marconi preferred to work by trial and error, and his father's servants were kept busy in the sweltering Italian summer digging holes to bury the metal plates that acted as grounds. By this painstaking method he found he could increase the range of reception by using longer antennas.

The use of antennas

Marconi found that copper wires mounted on a wooden pole provided a more effective and convenient antenna than a metal plate held high in the air. When he added an antenna to the receiver the transmission was greatly improved. The use of antennas on transmitters and receivers in all forms of wireless communication is still very important today.

The world's highest television antenna. It is located high in the Sandia Mountains near Albuquerque, New Mexico.

One day Marconi happened to have two receivers set up, one in front of a hill and one behind it. To his amazement he found that both receivers picked up the signal he transmitted. He believed at the time that the electromagnetic waves must have traveled through the hill, but we know today that the waves probably reached the other side of the hill because they were reflected off charged layers in the Earth's atmosphere.

Even though he was wrong about the route traveled by the waves, Marconi was absolutely right about the importance of his discovery. He had shown beyond doubt that it was possible to develop a system of wireless telegraphy over a useful range that was not affected by natural obstacles such as hills.

Marconi in 1896. He was twenty-two years old and had traveled to England to try to interest the authorities in his work on wireless communication.

Marconi was now twenty-one years old, and even his father was becoming impressed with his experiments. He gave him money to buy materials and equipment. Marconi wanted to offer his new invention to the Italian Government, but they already had a working system of overhead telegraph lines and submarine cables and did not think that a wireless system was necessary. This was a great disappointment to Marconi and his father, but his mother was not so discouraged. She felt that her son would have a better chance in England, where her relations would be able to arrange the necessary introductions. So, in February 1896, Marconi set off with his mother for England with luggage for a long stay and two large trunks filled with wireless equipment.

A

L896.

No. 12039.

VICTORIA, BY THE GRACE OF GOD,

Of the United Kingdom of Great Britain and Ireland, Queen, Defender of the Faith: To all to whom these presents shall come, Greeting:

WHEREAS GUGLIELMO MARCONI of 71 Hereford Road Bayswater in the County of Middlesex,————

hath represented unto us that he is in possession of an invention for

Improvements in transmitting electrical impulses and signals and in apparatus therefor,

that he is the true and first inventor thereof, and that the same is not in use by any other person, to the best of his knowledge and belief:

AND WHEREAS the said inventor hath humbly prayed that We would be graciously pleased to grant unto him (hereinafter, together with his executors, administrators, and assigns, or any of them, referred to as the said patentee) our Royal Letters Patent for the sole use and advantage of his said invention:

AND WHEREAS the said inventor hath by and in his complete specification particularly described the nature of his said invention:

AND WHEREAS we, being willing to encourage all inventions which may be for the public good, are graciously pleased to condescend to his request:

KNOW YE THEREFORE, that We, of our especial grace, certain knowledge, and mere motion, do by these presents, for us, our heirs and successors, give and grant unto the said patentee our especial license, full power, sole privilege, and authority that the said patentee, by himself, his agents, or licensees, and no others, may at all times hereafter, during the term of years herein mentioned, make, use, exercise, and vend the said invention within our United Kingdom of Great Britain and Ireland and Isle of Man in such manner as to him or them may seem meet, and that the said patentee shall have and enjoy the whole profit and advantage from time to time accruing by reason of the said invention during the term of fourteen years from the date hereunder written of these presents: AND to the end that the said patentee may have and enjoy the sole use and exercise, and the full benefit of the said invention, We do by these presents, for us, our heirs and successors, strictly command all our subjects whatsoever, within our United Kingdom of Great Britain and Ireland and the Isle of Man, that they do not at any time during the continuance of the said term of fourteen years, either directly or indirectly, make use of, or put in practice, the said invention, or any part of

the same, nor in anywise imitate the same, nor make, or cause to be made, any addition thereto or subtraction therefrom, whereby to pretend themselves the inventors thereof, without the consent, license, or agreement of the said patentee in writing under his hand and seal, on pain of incurring such penalties as may be justly inflicted on such offenders for their contempt of this our Royal command, and of being answerable to the patentee according to law for his damages thereby occasioned:

PROVIDED that these our letters patent are on this condition: that if at any time during the said term it be made to appear to us, our heirs or successors, or any six or more of our Privy Council, that this our grant is contrary to law, or prejudicial or inconvenient to our subjects in general, or that the said invention is not a new invention as to the public use and exercise thereof within our United Kingdom of Great Britain and Ireland and Isle of Man, or that the said patentee is not the first and true inventor thereof within this realm as aforesaid, these our letters patent shall forthwith determine, and be void to all intents and purposes, notwithstanding anything hereinbefore contained: PROVIDED ALSO, that if the said patentee shall not pay all fees by law required to be paid in respect of the grant of these letters patent, or in respect of any matter relating thereto, at the time or times and in manner for the time being by law provided; and also if the said patentee shall not supply, or cause to be supplied for our service all such articles of the said invention as may be required by the officers or commissioners administering any department of our service, in such manner, at such times, and at and upon such reasonable prices and terms as shall be settled in manner for the time being by law provided, then, and in any of the said cases, these our letters patent, and all privileges and advantages whatever hereby granted, shall determine and become void, notwithstanding anything hereinbefore contained: PROVIDED ALSO, that nothing herein contained shall prevent the granting of licenses in such manner and for such considerations as they may by law be granted: AND lastly, we do by these presents, for us, our heirs and successors, grant unto the said patentee that these our letters patent shall be construed in the most beneficial sense for the advantage of the said patentee.

IN WITNESS whereof we have caused these our letters to be made patent this second day of June, one thousand eight hundred and ninety-six, and to be sealed as of the second day of June, one thousand eight hundred and ninety-six.

C. N. DALTON,

Comptroller-General of Patents.

One of Marconi's first aims when he arrived in England was to patent his invention. He was awarded a patent on June 2, 1896. This was the first patent ever issued for wireless telegraphy.

Marconi's first entry into Britain with his wireless equipment was not very promising. Suspicious customs officials were so puzzled by the strange apparatus that they insisted on taking it apart before they would let it pass. Thus his first job in England was to reassemble his damaged equipment.

After spending some weeks repairing and improving his equipment, Marconi applied for a patent for it. This was the first patent ever issued for wireless telegraphy. With the help of one of his mother's relatives, he then set about demonstrating his wireless telegraphy system to a number of influential people. William Preece, the chief engineer of the General Post Office, was most impressed by the invention and agreed to do all he could to promote it.

AN HOTEL FOR BERLIN.

of a Colossal Structure to be Run on Our Lines.

CONRIED AND BOYD AT ODDS IN STOCKS

Opera Director's Brother Handled the Dealings of the Opera House Superintendent.

PROFIT FIGURES WIDE APART

$40,000, Says Boyd, Perhaps $300, Says Conried, and He'll Pay in Due Time.

FIRST WIRELESS PRESS MESSAGE ACROSS THE ATLANTIC

Signalizing the Opening of the Marconi Service to the Public, and Conveying a Message of Congratulation from Privy Councillor Baron Avebury, Formerly Sir John Lubbock.

THE WESTERN UNION TELEGRAPH COMPANY.

24,000 OFFICES IN AMERICA. CABLE SERVICE TO ALL THE WORLD.

RECEIVED at 313 Sixth Ave. Corner 46th St.
TELEPHONE: 3907 BRYANT.

London Via Marconi Wireless Glace Bay N S Oct 17th,

Times, New York.

This message marks opening transatlantic wireless handed Marconi company for transmission Ireland Breton limited 50 words only send one many messages received Times signalize event quote trust introduction wireless more closely unite people states Great Britian who seem form one Nation though under two Governments and whose interests are really identical.

Avebury Marshall .... 1210 Am Oct17th

ALWAYS OPEN. MONEY TRANSFERRED BY TELEGRAPH. CABLE OFFICE.

The above message was immediately followed by others which appear in another column of The Times this morning.

MARCONI CONGRATULATES THE NEW YORK TIMES

GLACE BAY, NOVA SCOTIA, Oct. 17.—Mr. Marconi says: "Congratulate New York Times on having received first westward press message."

FROM THE PRIME MINISTER OF FRANCE.

WIRELESS JOINS TWO WORLDS

Marconi Transatlantic Service Opened with a Dispatch to The New York Times.

MESSAGES FROM EMINENT MEN

Prime Minister Clemenceau, the Duke of Argyll, Lord Avebury and Others Send Greetings.

10,000 WORDS THE FIRST DAY

Marconi in Personal Supervision at Glace Bay and Greatly Pleased with the Results.

SIR HIRAM MAXIM'S TRIBUTE

His Message to Peter Cooper Hewitt in New York, Who Is Trying to Pick Up the Oversea Messages.

By Marconi Transatlantic Wireless Telegraph to The New York Times.

LONDON, Oct. 17.—This message marks the opening of the transatlantic wireless service. It is handed to the Marconi Company here for transmission to Ireland, and thence to Cape Breton, Nova Scotia, and New York. As it is limited to fifty words, I can send at present only one of the many messages received for transmission to The New York Times to signalize the event. This message, from Privy Councillor Lord Ave-

---

After several successful demonstrations of the equipment in London for Post Office officials, Marconi gave a demonstration in front of military and naval observers. They recognized the value of the new system for communication, especially between ships at sea. Marconi continued to improve his system and was soon able to send wireless signals across the Bristol Channel, a distance of 8 miles (13 km). This was the first time wireless signals had been sent over water.

The general public became aware of Marconi's work when William Preece gave a lecture to the British Association, an organization devoted to science and technology. At the lecture Preece held a transmitter while Marconi walked around the room carrying a

The headlines in The New York Times *of October 18, 1907, announcing the first wireless message across the Atlantic. This breakthrough was made thirty years after Marconi's arrival in England.*

receiver. Whenever Preece pressed the transmitting key, a bell rang in Marconi's receiver. The lecture caused a sensation and the next day the name "Marconi" was in the newspaper headlines.

Marconi now worried that others might try to exploit his invention. He had always imagined that the idea of using electromagnetic waves for wireless communication was "so elementary, so simple in logic, that it seemed difficult for me to believe that no one else had thought of putting it into practice." To protect his system against competitors he decided to set up in business. With the help of his cousin, he established The Wireless Telegraph and Signal Company Limited on July 20, 1897. The Company was later renamed the Marconi Company, and shares were sold to the public.

Only a little more than a year after his arrival in England, Marconi had successfully demonstrated and patented his equipment and set up his own company.

Marconi shortly after his arrival in England. He is shown here with his transmitter and receiver.

4 Wireless Goes International

Marconi left Italy for England because the Italian Government was not interested in making use of his invention. But now that he had been able to provide spectacular examples of wireless communication, the Italian Government had a change of heart. In 1897, when Marconi was twenty-three, the Minister of the Italian Navy invited him to return to Italy to demonstrate his equipment.

Marconi returned to his native land in triumph. He was presented to the King and Queen of Italy, who congratulated him on his work. The press reported his every move in great detail, and for once, Marconi's father glowed with pride at his son's achievements. When Marconi returned to his home he was treated as the guest of honor rather than as a troublesome child who wasted time and money carrying out harebrained experiments in the attic.

Marconi had always remained loyal to his native country and was delighted to have the chance to show the Italian Government how his wireless system worked. As a mark of his patriotism, the first message he transmitted to demonstrate his system was *Viva l'Italia!* He went on to show how wireless communication could be used to reach ships at sea, and for the first time wireless messages were received by ships that were far out of sight beyond the horizon.

Marconi's visit to Italy was a great success and was reported by newspapers all over Italy. The English papers also followed Marconi's progress with interest and, as a result, he was even more famous when he returned to England than he had been when he left. But Marconi did not let fame go to his head and he continued to work to improve his system. When he returned to England, one of his first projects was to set

Opposite *Marconi's wireless proved to be very useful for communication at sea. Here, a Marconi wireless telegraph is being used to report the results of an international yacht race.*

Marconi—from a Photograph.

The Coherer.

Diagram of the Transmitter and Receiver.

up an antenna 130 feet (40 m) high outside the Needles Hotel on the Isle of Wight, in order to test reception at sea. The weather was stormy, and the small ship Marconi hired to carry the receiving equipment was tossed about and flooded with water. In spite of the dangerous conditions Marconi was able to send messages over a range of almost 20 miles (32 km). This proved once and for all that his equipment was capable of working even under difficult conditions at sea.

Marconi also set up regular demonstrations in which he transmitted messages to the mainland. The famous British physicist Lord Kelvin, who had once expressed doubts about Marconi's system, was so impressed by these demonstrations that he insisted on sending several messages to his friends and paying Marconi a shilling for each message. This was the first time wireless messages had ever been sent commercially.

Up until now, Marconi's wireless links had been mainly in and around England. To be really successful the system had to be capable of communicating internationally. His first goal was to send messages between England and France. In March 1899 the French finally agreed to set up a wireless station at Wimereux, on the coast near Boulogne. Just a few weeks later, the first messages were sent to and received from France.

The value of the wireless system was now well established, but Marconi had an even larger goal in mind. He dreamed of sending messages by wireless across the Atlantic Ocean. Many scientists thought Marconi's dream was crazy. The distance was more than twenty times greater than his longest transmission and, because the surface of the ocean is not flat, the electromagnetic waves would have to travel over a huge mountain of water. But Marconi was not discouraged. He believed that, because transmission beyond the horizon was possible, the range of the signals was limited only by the power of the transmitter.

Opposite *The first international wireless station at Wimereux, near Boulogne, on the coast of France. In 1899 the first international wireless messages were sent between England and France.*

Electromagnetic waves

The link with France provided valuable scientific evidence about the way electromagnetic waves travel. Some of the signals sent from Boulogne were unexpectedly received at a station set up in Chelmsford, over 80 miles (129 km) away. This was definite proof that electromagnetic waves could travel beyond the horizon, but it was to be many years before scientists understood why. We now know the waves can be reflected off electrically charged layers in the Earth's upper atmosphere. As a result they can travel over very long distances in a series of "skips," like a flat stone skipping over the surface of the water.

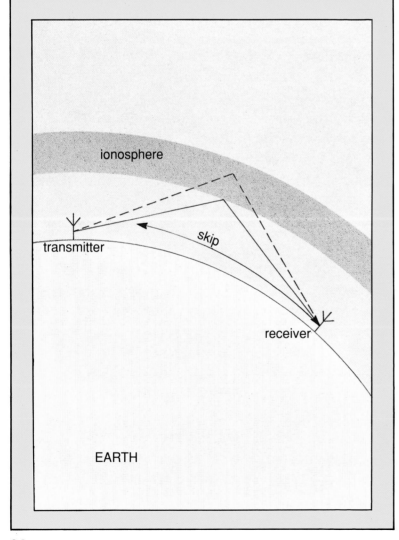

A diagram showing how electromagnetic waves are reflected off the electrically charged layers in the Earth's upper atmosphere. This is shown, simply, as one layer: the ionosphere.

He chose a remote site on the south coast of Britain, at Poldhu in Cornwall, to build his first high-power transmitter. Marconi stayed in Cornwall to supervise the building of the station and sent one of his assistants to Cape Cod, on the east coast of the United States, to build the second station. Both stations included a large antenna, which was made up of twenty very tall poles up to 215 feet (65.5 m) high. These were connected to each other by a complicated arrangement of wires. The building of these antennas proved to be Marconi's biggest challenge. First, strong winds at Cape Cod blew down one antenna, then a great storm at Poldhu destroyed the other.

Marconi decided to abandon plans for a transmitting station in the United States and to settle for one-way

The wireless station at Poldhu in Cornwall, England. The first wireless signals across the Atlantic were sent from Poldhu to Newfoundland in Canada on December 12, 1901.

communication between Poldhu and the nearest point in North America: Newfoundland, Canada. Instead of building the usual kind of station in Newfoundland, he decided to use kites and balloons to support a wire antenna. In Newfoundland, the governor allowed him to use an empty building for his experiments.

Marconi cabled Poldhu to begin transmitting "dot dot dot," the Morse code for the letter S, for three hours every day. The weather was very stormy, and several kites and balloons were lost when his assistants tried to raise the antenna. Meanwhile, Marconi sat anxiously straining to hear the faint "dot dot dot" through his earphones. On December 12, 1901, he heard the signals through the roar of the naturally occurring radio noise. He cautiously asked his assistant to listen, and he too could just hear the faint transmission. Wireless

In Newfoundland, Marconi decided to use kites and balloons to support his antennas rather than taking the time to build masts. Here Marconi's team is working to raise one of the antennas on a kite.

Canada to England. Dec: 5ʰ 1902. First tape signals received.

A log book recording the arrival of the first transatlantic signals sent from Newfoundland, Canada, to Poldhu in England.

signals had been transmitted across the Atlantic for the first time.

When Marconi announced his achievement the public was thrilled. However, some scientists wondered whether Marconi's ears had deceived him. Marconi soon put their doubts to rest when he set up a large antenna on a transatlantic ship traveling from Europe to the United States and was able to receive messages from Poldhu at distances of 1,550 miles (2,494 km). He received congratulations from all over the world. The American inventor Thomas Edison called him "the young man who succeeded in jumping an electric wave clear across the Atlantic Ocean."

Marconi hoped to set up a regular transatlantic wireless service, but he soon found that reception was not reliable enough for this. Instead he decided to use his system to provide a long-range communication and news service for ships at sea. By the following year, seventy ships were equipped with Marconi wireless equipment and there were twenty-five land stations.

The marine service was a great success and captured the imagination of the public, especially when, in 1910,

31

it was used to help capture the notorious murderer Dr. Crippen, who had tried to escape across the Atlantic on a passenger liner. Wireless was also responsible for saving many lives when the "unsinkable" liner, the *Titanic*, struck an iceberg in 1912 and sank.

In 1905 Marconi married a beautiful young Irish girl, Beatrice O'Brien. She must have been very surprised when one of the first things he did was to take her with him to his remote station at Glace Bay in Nova Scotia, Canada, to help him work on improvements to his transatlantic wireless link.

This must have been a difficult time for Beatrice, but for Marconi it was a very creative one. While

Marconi's wireless helped to capture the notorious murderer Dr. Crippen as he tried to escape across the Atlantic on a passenger liner.

Beatrice O' Brien, the young Irish girl who married Marconi in 1905.

experimenting, Marconi noticed that an antenna wire lying on the ground received transmitted signals better when its free end pointed away from the transmitter. This observation led to the development of what he called the "inverted-L aerial," because the horizontal part of the antenna was much longer than the vertical part and made the antenna look like a capital letter L lying on its side. This type of antenna not only received better but also transmitted more efficiently, and turned out to be a great breakthrough in long-range communications. At this time Marconi also found a better way of transmitting the radio signals by more precisely controlling the spark that broadcast the radio waves from the transmitting antenna.

Marconi sitting near a wireless operator in his remote wireless station in Glace Bay, Nova Scotia, Canada. In 1907, a transatlantic wireless service was set up between Glace Bay and Clifden.

With these two new improvements Marconi felt ready to offer a commercial service, transmitting messages by wireless across the Atlantic Ocean. Unfortunately, his ambitious plans ran into difficulties. The system did not work very reliably, and customers became dissatisfied. In addition, the Marconi Company was short of money, and it became necessary to find a new manager quickly in order to keep the company going.

But all was not gloomy for Marconi during this difficult period. The birth of a daughter in 1908 was a joyous event. In 1909, Marconi, who had never even received a University degree, shared the Nobel Prize for Physics for his work on wireless communication with another radio pioneer, Professor Karl Ferdinand Braun. The year 1910 was also a happy one, with the birth of his son. And, thanks to better management, the Marconi Company was now profitable again.

5 Wireless Around the World

Having conquered the Atlantic, Marconi dreamed of setting up an "Imperial Wireless Scheme," a network of stations to link the entire British Empire. The British Government was quick to see the value of the plan. After all, wireless waves would not be affected if an unfriendly foreign country decided to damage overland telegraph wires, or if an enemy ship cut an underwater cable. However, they were very worried about the fact that the Marconi Company alone would build and control this vital communication link. Eventually, a compromise was reached whereby the British Government would own the stations and pay the Marconi Company a fee to use them. The first stations were eventually begun in 1913, but the project was abandoned in 1914, when World War I plunged Europe into chaos.

A Beam System transmitting station in Grimsby, England, in 1927. The Beam network linked the world via shortwave stations that transmitted messages in Morse code. This system could have been introduced much earlier, had it not been for World War I (1914–18).

In 1912, Marconi and Beatrice took a motoring holiday to Italy. What was meant to be a happy, relaxing trip turned into a near tragedy, when their automobile collided head-on with another. Beatrice was not badly hurt, but Marconi lost an eye in the accident. After this narrow escape, he returned to Britain more determined than ever to carry on with his work.

In July 1914, the British King, George V, recognized Marconi's achievements when he presented him with the honorary title of Knight Grand Cross of the Royal Victorian Order. But a month later, with the outbreak of World War I, Marconi found that, as a foreigner, he

After the outbreak of World War I, Marconi joined the Italian forces as an advisor on radio communication. He was soon appointed Chief of the Wireless Department of the Italian Army.

was viewed with suspicion and his movements were restricted in his adopted home.

He returned to Italy, where he took a seat in the Italian Senate. When Italy joined the war on the Allied side, Marconi joined the Italian forces as an advisor on radio communications. His work during the war led to great advances in the use of radio waves for navigation and in wireless communication for military aircraft. He also worked on a system of ship-to-ship communication over small distances using short-waves. This work eventually led to a worldwide communications system.

The war years were busy ones for Marconi. In addition to his work with radio communications, he also served as a diplomat, representing Italy abroad and serving as a delegate to the Paris Peace Conference in 1919.

After the war ended, Marconi returned to his work on wireless communication with great enthusiasm. He bought a large yacht from the British Navy and equipped it with a laboratory for his radio experiments. He called his yacht the *Elettra* and made it a comfortable base where he could both work and relax.

Marconi in the radio room on his yacht Elettra.

6 Shortwaves to Travel Long Distances

After the war, Marconi continued with his plan to make wireless communication possible throughout the world. His first idea was to develop very powerful stations to transmit long waves over thousands of miles. In 1924, the Marconi Company received orders for high-powered long-wave stations from Australia and South Africa. But before the stations were started Marconi began work on a new idea: long-distance transmission using shortwaves.

The waves which Marconi had used in his transatlantic service had wavelengths of several thousand yards and it was necessary to build very high-powered and expensive stations in order to transmit the waves over long distances. In contrast, shortwaves, which have wavelengths of less than 1,000 feet (300 m), can be sent using relatively inexpensive and low-powered transmitters.

The electromagnetic spectrum stretches from the very short wavelengths of gamma rays to the much longer wavelengths of radio waves.

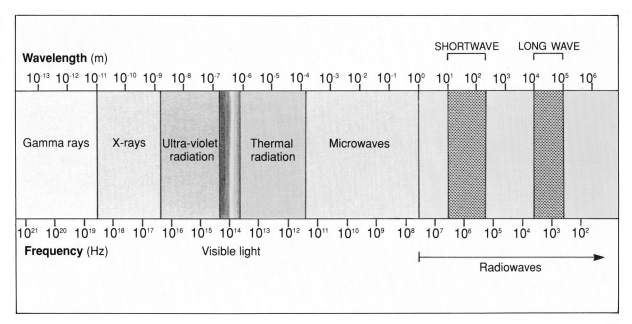

At first Marconi thought that shortwaves could only travel over short distances. He soon began to receive many reports of shortwave transmissions being received much farther away than expected. He used radio receivers on his yacht to confirm these reports. For some of his tests he sailed the *Elettra* to a location 2,500 miles (4,000 km) away from the shortwave transmitter at Poldhu. There he found that at night he could receive shortwave signals more strongly than long-wave signals transmitted from a similar distance. This surprised him because the long waves were transmitted using much greater amounts of power. We know now that shortwaves can travel so far using low-power transmitters because they bounce off electrically charged layers in the Earth's atmosphere, rather than traveling over the Earth's surface.

Marconi's experiments with shortwave reception on the *Elettra* convinced him that shortwaves held the key to his dream of linking the British Empire. The British Government was more cautious, but agreed to let the Marconi Company build a series of shortwave stations throughout the Empire. The agreement was made with the understanding that if the system was a failure, the Marconi Company would bear all the cost. This was one of the biggest risks Marconi had ever taken in his business career. But he was so confident that he agreed to the Government's terms and a contract was signed in 1924.

One by one the stations were built and by 1926 several were put into operation. It soon became clear that the new system was a resounding success. The network was named the Beam System because it used highly directional antennas, which are also known as beam antennas. This type of antenna concentrates, or focuses, signals in one direction. Marconi's childhood dream of worldwide communication using radio waves had become a reality.

Although the engineers at the Marconi Company had to work very quickly to design the equipment for the beam stations, the equipment they built remained in use for many years. In fact, nearly forty years later, when the Science Museum in London asked the Marconi Company for one of the original beam transmitters to use in an exhibition, they were told they had to wait until the transmitter could be released from service. The Beam System transmitted messages in Morse code and was used for many years, but today long-range radio transmitters that transmit speech are more common.

A Marconi beam transmitter and receiver. This equipment was so well designed that it remained in use for more than forty years.

Around this time, engineers at the Marconi Company in Chelmsford were looking at ways of transmitting speech and music using radio waves. They were also developing home radio receivers to allow people to tune in to the broadcasts. In 1920, the Marconi Company presented the first advertised public program broadcast "over the air." In 1922, the Marconi Company joined five other British companies, interested in providing wireless entertainment, to form the British Broadcasting Company. This was the forerunner of the BBC, Britain's main broadcasting organization.

By 1922, the public enthusiasm for "listening in" to radio broadcasts was growing. The picture shows one of the early Marconi home receivers.

7 The Last Years

While Marconi worked on his wireless inventions he found less and less time to spend with his wife, Beatrice. Finally, in 1924, they decided to separate. But although his work seemed to be all-absorbing, Marconi missed family life, and in 1926 he re-married. He and his new wife, Cristina, made their home in Italy, and four years later his third daughter was born.

During this time Marconi began to suffer heart attacks. His doctors recommended rest and relaxation, but Marconi's mind was still teeming with ideas that he wanted to test. He was never happy unless he was working on his latest experiments.

Marconi was now becoming interested in microwaves, waves with wavelengths of less than a yard. He soon realized that microwaves could be very

The radar equipment on the British Frigate HMS Yarmouth. *Radar is considered an essential piece of equipment on most modern Navy and Merchant ships, to ensure safe navigation when visibility is poor.*

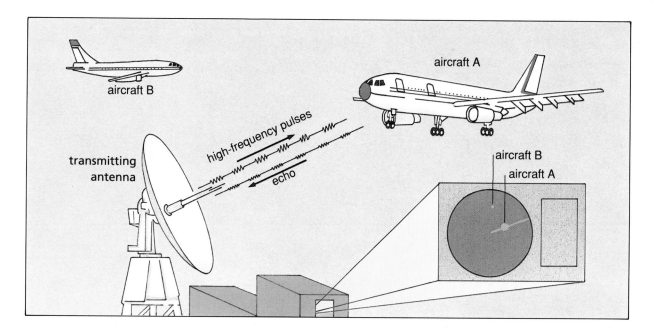

Labels in image: aircraft B, aircraft A, transmitting antenna, high-frequency pulses, echo, aircraft B, aircraft A

useful. For example, microwaves can be sent in a very narrow beam toward the receiving antenna and this means that communication links can be made more private. Even more important, he found that because microwaves do not bend as they travel through the air, they could be used to help ships find their way into harbors in fog or bad weather. He designed a system that used two separate transmitters to send microwaves out toward the sea. The beams were aimed so that they overlapped slightly just at the harbor entrance. If the ship was located on either side of this line, its receiver detected a sound, but when the ship was moving along the line, there was no sound. In a dramatic demonstration of this system he covered all the windows on the bridge of his yacht *Elettra* and had the helmsman steam into a harbor at normal speed, guided only by the microwave beacon he had installed on the cliffs.

When he was working on this system Marconi noticed that if an object, such as an automobile or another ship, passed through the beam, a hissing noise was heard through the receiver. This observation led to the development of radar, a method of detecting ships and airplanes using microwaves.

A diagram showing a modern radar system. The radio-wave pulses sent out by the transmitter "bounce" back from the aircraft. These reflected pulses are picked up by a receiver. They are interpreted to show the relative positions of the aircraft.

Marconi continued working on his wireless system until he died.

In addition to his scientific work, Marconi continued to represent Italy abroad. These trips were very tiring, and Marconi's health continued to weaken. He died on July 20, 1937, at his home in Rome, at the age of sixty-three.

Wireless carried the news of his death all over the world. Many famous statesmen and scientists praised Marconi's accomplishments, newspapers wrote about his achievements, and flags were flown at half-mast in the great capitals of the world. Many Italians stood for hours in the heat of the Roman summer to pay their respects. But the greatest tribute of all was paid by the operators of wireless stations around the world: they stopped all transmission for two minutes. For those two minutes the airwaves were once again silent, just as they had been before the Italian pioneer in telecommunications achieved his boyhood dream of sending wireless messages all over the world.

Date Chart

1874   (April 25) Guglielmo Marconi born in Bologna, Italy.

1894   Marconi has the idea of using electromagnetic waves for transmitting messages without wires.

1895   He discovers the use of antennas to extend the range of transmission and transmits his first messages over a hill.

1896   (February) Travels to England to try to develop his wireless system.

1896   (June 2) Is granted the world's first wireless telegraphy patent.

1897   (July) The Wireless Telegraph and Signal Company, later the Marconi Company, is registered. Marconi returns to Italy to demonstrate his system to the Italian Government.

1899   (March) First international wireless link between Wimereux near Boulogne in northern France and Dover in England is established.

1899   (September) Marconi demonstrates that radio wave reception is not restricted to line of sight.

1900   Decides to try to send radio signals across the Atlantic. Wireless equipment is installed on a merchant ship for the first time.

1901   (December 12) At his base in Newfoundland, Marconi picks up signals transmitted from Poldhu, England, for the first time.

1909   Awarded the Nobel Prize for Physics, jointly with Karl Ferdinand Braun.

1910   The Marconi Company submits proposals to the British Government to build a network of channels to link the British Empire.

1912   Marconi loses an eye in an automobile accident in Italy.

1914   (September) Marconi returns to Italy and serves in the Italian Government and armed services.

1920   (June 15) Britain's first advertised public broadcast.

1922   The Marconi Company joins with other companies to form the British Broadcasting Company.

1924   The Marconi Company proposes the "Imperial Wireless Scheme" based on shortwaves (the Beam System).

1934   Marconi demonstrates the use of ultrahigh-frequency waves for navigation.

1935   Demonstrates the principles of radar.

1937   (July 20) Marconi dies at the age of sixty-three.

Books to Read

Audio & Radio by Robert Hawkins (EDC. 1982)

On the Air: Radio Broadcasting by Robert Hawkins (Messner, 1984)

Radio and Radar by Frank Young (Watts, 1984)

Radio: From Marconi to the Space Age by Alden R. Carter (Watts, 1987)

Glossary

Antenna (originally called an aerial) A device used to launch radio signals into space from a transmitter and to gather them up at a radio receiver.

Broadcasts Transmissions of radio waves intended to be received by the public.

Charged layers Layers in the Earth's atmosphere that have electrical charges. The layers become electrically charged because they are exposed to radiation from the Sun. Many wavelengths of radio waves are bounced, or reflected, off these layers.

Coil A length of wire wound into concentric circles, like a spring, used to increase the strength of an electromagnetic force. A coil is able to store an amount of electricity and release it again, just as a stretched piece of elastic springs back when the ends are released.

Contact A switch for making and breaking an electrical circuit.

Detector A device for recognizing the presence of electrical currents.

Electromagnetic waves Rapidly changing electrical and magnetic forces that originate from atoms and molecules and travel as waves. Electromagnetic waves are caused by the displacement of electric and magnetic forces in the same way as water waves are caused by the displacement of water.

Ground A wire that is used to carry electrical current into the ground and draw it safely away. It prevents dangerous sparks.

Long waves Radio waves that have wavelengths between 3,280 and 32,800 feet (1,000 and 10,000 m). These waves bend and flow over the surface of the Earth and travel over the horizon. Very powerful transmitters are needed to transmit long waves over great distances.

Patent The exclusive right to make or sell a new invention.

Resistance A property that reduces the flow of electricity in a material.

Shortwaves Radio waves that have wavelengths between 33 and 985 feet (10 and 300 m). They travel over long distances by bouncing off electrically charged layers in the Earth's atmosphere. They can be transmitted all over the world using relatively low-power transmitters.

Theory An explanation of how something works.

Transmission The sending out of radio waves.

Transmitter The device used to send out, or transmit, radio waves. Transmitters can be very simple. The earliest transmitters consisted of a coil of wire connected to the terminals of a battery and to two copper plates. When the electrical circuit was complete, it made a spark jump across a small gap.

Vacuum An empty space that is not occupied by any solids, liquids or gases.

Velocity Speed in a particular direction.

Wavelength The distance from one point on a wave to an identical point on the next wave.

Picture acknowledgments

The author and publishers would like to thank the following for allowing illustrations to be reproduced in this book: Mary Evans *front cover, frontispiece*, 26, 33, 36/37, 45; GEC/Marconi 7, 12, 18, 21, 22, 23, 30, 35, 42; Michael Holford 9; Ann Ronan 25, 29; Science Photo Library 6, 19, 43; Wayland Picture Library 4, 5, 8, 11, 14, 20, 31, 32, 34, 38, 41. Cover artwork is by Richard Hook. All inside artwork is by Jenny Hughes.

Index